# Having Nothing
# Lacking Nothing

Oh Lis,
This calling
on us to share
the stories the Lord
has entrusted to us —
what a blessing this
calling brings!

Melanie DeKruyter

Love,
Melanie

*This book is dedicated to John, my home.*

WinePress Publishing (PO Box 428, Enumclaw, WA 98022) functions only as book publisher. As such, the ultimate design, content, editorial accuracy, and views expressed or implied in this work are those of the author.

Unless otherwise noted, all Scriptures are taken from the *New American Standard Bible*®, © 1960, 1962, 1963, 1968, 1971, 1972, 1973, 1975, 1977, 1995 by The Lockman Foundation. Used by permission. (www. Lockman.org)

ISBN 13: 978-1-57921-994-9
ISBN 10: 1-57921-994-2
Library of Congress Catalog Card Number: 2008938367

# Contents

Prologue: His Doing And Undoing ......................... v

1. Desert ................................................ 1
2. Immovable Rock ....................................... 5
3. Holes in the Text .................................... 9
4. Shelter ............................................. 13
5. Sanctuary: His Dwelling Place ...................... 17
6. Sanctuary: The Sabbath ............................. 21
7. Holy of Holies ..................................... 25
8. Yad Vashem ......................................... 31
9. Reconstruction ..................................... 35
10. Faith Undone ...................................... 39
11. Aqueducts in the Sand ............................. 43
12. Mount Nebo ........................................ 47
13. Home Isn't ........................................ 51
14. Sin Cycle ......................................... 55
15. Who Do You Say That I Am? ......................... 59
16. Making Jesus ...................................... 63
17. Having Nothing, Lacking Nothing .................. 67
18. If Anyone Is Thirsty .............................. 73
19. The Best Is Yet ................................... 77
20. Leaving the Desert ................................ 81

Gratitude ............................................ 85

# Prologue
## His Doing And Undoing

My husband and I suspected we were in store for a remarkable adventure when we joined a group of fifty-six people chasing an energetic, passionate Bible scholar and teacher all over Israel and Turkey. We were not wrong, yet little did we know how much that study tour would change our lives.

We spent nearly three weeks treading ancient paths in the land of the Bible as our teacher introduced us to the geographical and cultural setting of the biblical story. We saw the land's striking beauty, awesome barren deserts, and numerous, amazing historic sites of land of the Bible. And we learned a great deal about the resilience and fortitude of the people who have called this land their home.

When we returned home to Michigan, I spent the next two years reflecting on what I discovered on that journey, but it barely scratched the surface of all we had been given during that time. I sought to unpack the stories we learned—stories rooted in real places and specific times in the Old and New Testaments of Scripture.

Understanding the context in which the biblical authors recorded God's stories, old and new, dramatically changed how I now read and embrace God's Word.

Two years after returning home, and a few months after our second daughter was born, our family moved to Jerusalem to live and study in the land and culture of the Bible. We expected simply to study hard and enjoy the beauty of the land, but the Lord had much more in mind for us.

Our adjustment to life in Israel was far more difficult than we ever anticipated. We could never have guessed how far God intended to move us away from ourselves and into Him, and we were amazed to experience the fullness of the truth that the Lord is a great deal more interested in who we are becoming than in what we know or accomplish.

We expected our training to deepen our understanding of Scripture, and it certainly did. *Having Nothing, Lacking Nothing* reflects on our experiences in the classroom as well as our archaeological field studies in Israel, the West Bank, and Jordan.

Studying archaeology gave me a new perspective on the Bible's historical accuracy and yet-remaining mysteries of many biblical places. Exploring the setting and cultural background of the ancient land illuminated the biblical account, which is so rich, and often obscure, in details about people and places. I found that my study of rabbinic Judaism provided fresh insight into Jesus' lifestyle, teaching, and heart.

These experiences provided a profoundly different and exciting perspective of God's interaction with the people in the biblical story than I had ever known.

While this book explores the many lessons learned in our studies, it is also a sharing of intimate moments with the Lord in both great and terrible times. Within days of moving to Jerusalem, it was clear God would waste no time in drawing us to Him. Our babies were not sleeping, and we were unaccustomed to the desert heat of August, which threatened their health and ours. As we began to feel some sense of settling in, tragedy struck back home. Flying back across the world appeared necessary and impossible.

This book will also reflect on the real struggles experienced while living in an often volatile place notorious for spiritual and political tension. The overwhelming responsibilities of full-time graduate work, of raising two young children, and of trying to thrive in a very foreign culture and unstable environment revealed a surprising parallel between how God sustained His people in biblical times and how he sustains us today.

I begin each chapter with a teaching or conversation that sent me to the Scriptures to understand how God intervened with people in biblical times. In seeking to hear the Lord's voice and gain His perspective, the Lord constantly provided glimpses into the ways He pulls us to Himself today.

As we struggled to survive spiritually and emotionally in the desolate landscape, the desert wanderings of the people of Israel came to life. According to my teaching rabbi, the Jewish people say Israel's time in the desert was a "honeymoon with God." Having nothing, yet lacking nothing, the Israelites had never experienced such intimacy with the Holy One—the record makes it clear they would struggle to keep that intimacy.

In leaving the desert for the land of promise, the Israelites found it increasingly difficult to cling to God as they slowly immersed themselves in a pagan culture of self-sufficiency. By leaving my comfortable life in the green meadows of Michigan for the deserts of Israel, I, too, have now lived in a place where the Lord's sustaining promises and constant presence were all I had.

Yet having nothing, I found we lacked nothing—despite losing loved ones far away, experiencing the challenges of living in a culture hostile to our beliefs, and suffering miscarriages in our time abroad. Now that we are back home in Michigan, our family is slowly reentering a culture that champions self-sufficiency, and I more fully understand the Israelites' undoing upon entering the land of promise. I, too, forget to cling to the God whose sustaining goodness was more real to me when it was all I had.

I cherish the time spent in the desert because it demanded a lifestyle of need and total dependence on God. I pray this collection of reflections will encourage readers to see dark times and brokenness as invitations to cling tightly to the One whose provision is total.

# Chapter 1

# Desert

am in the desert—physically, emotionally, spiritually.

Jerusalem is hot. Without the convenience of an air-conditioned vehicle, every errand sends us walking—twenty-five minutes in one hundred degree arid heat just to get a few groceries, and then hurry home before they spoil in the sun.

Why aren't there any trees here for some occasional shade? The scorching sun is hard on the girls' delicate skin and they are always soaked in sweat. I am perpetually thirsty. Can I possibly drink enough to keep nursing tiny Kate?

Our apartment is a fairly good size considering this crowded city, and thankfully it is nestled in one of the safest neighborhoods in Jerusalem. However, it sits on a steep hill, making it an exhausting climb pushing a stroller bearing two kids and groceries.

There are no window screens in the apartment, but we must open all the windows to catch even the slightest breeze. This invites the mysterious bugs that feast on the girls' tender flesh—as well as the ever-present dust. The floors are dusty. Everything is dusty. I miss taking the girls outside so Brynn can toddle around and Kate can sit on the grass. There is no grass.

Every night since we arrived, the girls have cried for hours. At five months old, Kate is exhausted, trying to reconcile being seven hours off-schedule. Still months from turning two, Brynn wakes up screaming, trembling, and begs, "Go bye-bye." She clings to us dripping with tears and sweat, points to her car seat in the corner, and sobs, "All done, new bed . . . airplane . . . home . . . church . . . see kids." My sweet girl barely makes sentences, but nevertheless she is quite clear: she misses her home, her bed, and seeing her friends at church.

Other kids living nearby quickly lose interest because Brynn speaks only a few words, and these are not in their language. Mostly, she is alone, watching others play without her, and she is confused. It breaks my heart and John's.

The girls lie in bed and cry, and I lie in bed and cry, and ask, "What have we done? Why did we come here?" In my mind, I know the answers to both questions. But in my heart, I ache for clarity and rest.

John and I have been obedient, which fuels the anger in my frustration over these struggles. We answered this very recent, unexpected call to move to Israel to study the Word and get to know God better through the culture, history, and geography of the land of the Bible. Classes start soon; we desperately need sleep, not to mention a babysitter. How can I study? Has the Lord brought me here to raise the girls alone while my husband disappears into his coursework? I have never felt as lonely as I do right here and now.

My classes haven't started, but my education certainly has. I have learned that when my path brings me to the desert, I will face the evil one. The enemy knows I will either desperately seek my own way or choose to draw nearer to the Lord. This choice emerges in nearly every story of the Bible, and now this choice is mine—do I take matters into my own hands, or trust them in the Lord's?

The enemy whispers lies to me suggesting God brought me here and abandoned me, or that I am hurting my children by being here, or even that John will be too busy studying to be my companion. These lies signal my choice to withdraw in fear or draw near to the Source of life.

I am learning the life-giving essence of a loving community and the immeasurable value of pointing one another to truth in dark times. In these first, disheartening days we have heard encouraging words from our friends back home, who remind us we are loved and prayed for. These words have truly brought the sweet breath of God into my broken heart and anguished spirit.

Our community in Michigan is God's provision for us here. Without it, I may stand in this desert, forget the truth, and withdraw to wither and die in the scorching heat.

If I did not believe God has a community here that we will soon be part of, I would put both girls in their car seats and go home. There is no endeavor, not even the study of the biblical text, that could be of greater value than *living the Text in community* with people who love God.

It is in the Text that the Lord speaks directly to me and extinguishes the lies of the enemy. The Lord's Word is truly living water when I am dying of thirst:

> O Lord, You have searched me and known me,
> You know when I sit down and when I rise up;
> You understand my thought from afar.
> You scrutinize my path and my lying down,
> And are intimately acquainted with all my ways.
> Even before there is a word on my tongue,
> Behold, O Lord, You know it all.
> You have enclosed me behind and before,
> And laid Your hand upon me.
> Such knowledge is too wonderful for me;
> It is too high, I cannot attain it.
>
> —Psalm 139:1–6

So here I stand at the crossroads found in every desert. I have been so distracted by the seeming disorder in the current circumstances that I am in danger of missing what God has graciously put in place. If I dwell only on the absence of all we left behind, I cannot embrace a new community, nor will I seek a newfound dependence on the Lord.

I do not believe I am being punished because, after all, obedience brought me here. I do not believe I am being tested, though I suspect my faith will be getting a workout. I can either walk this path by sight, or I can walk by faith in what I cannot yet see.

# Chapter 2

# Immovable Rock

There was a man who walked the same road every day from his home to go into town. The path was uneven and rocky, making the uphill climb slippery as well. Every day as he walked he passed an enormous boulder. It was nearly as tall as he was, and each time he saw it, he marveled at its size.

One day as he approached this boulder, the man heard the voice of the Holy One, blessed be He, say, "Eliezar." He stopped, fell to his knees, lowered his head, and whispered, "Lord?"

The Holy One said, "Eliezar, there is something I want you to do for me."

Eliezar whispered reverently, "Yes, Lord, anything."

The Lord said to Eliezar, "Do you see that large boulder you walk by each day, always astonished at its size? I know you come this way every morning, and every morning, I want you to push against this boulder with all your might."

So every day Eliezar walked to town, and each morning he stopped at the boulder and put his shoulder to it. With all his strength he pushed, until his legs ached, his arms ached, and he could no longer bear the pain in his back. He pushed until he could push no more.

One morning, many months later, Eliezar had just put his shoulder to the rock when another voice spoke to him. "Eliezar. What are you doing, Eliezar?" It was the enemy, cursed be he, who interrupted him.

Eliezar stopped pushing, and replied, "I am pushing on this boulder, just as the Holy One has asked."

"But why?" asked the intruding voice. "Can't you see it is not doing any good? Every day you walk here, on this difficult road. Isn't it enough that you must climb that slippery, rocky hill to reach this place? And then you push on this rock, and look at it—has it moved even an inch?"

Eliezar stopped and looked, and certainly the rock had not moved. *Why was I thinking I could move it?* he wondered. Eliezar left the boulder and went on his way. The next day as he walked he reached the same spot and paused. He looked again at the rock, then left it and continued on his way. Soon, he no longer even noticed the boulder as he passed by.

Some time later, as Eliezar walked the familiar uphill path, the Holy One, blessed be He, gently called to him, "Eliezar."

Eliezar stopped, again fell to his knees, bowed his head, and said, "Lord, I am here."

"Eliezar, why are you about to walk past this boulder? Have I not asked you to push on it?"

Eliezar said, "Lord, for months I did just as you asked. And look—it has done no good. I push with all my might and arrive at my destination even dirtier and sweatier than before. And nothing has changed."

The Lord said, "Eliezar, you are not looking where I look. Open your eyes and look now at your arms. See the new muscle you have for working in your business? And your back, have you noticed the great strength you have gained in your back? And Eliezar, your legs, see how strong they are? Have you noticed how much easier your daily walk has become?"

Eliezar felt his arms, his back, his legs, and realized they were indeed much stronger than before.

The Lord said, "Eliezar, I did not ask you to move the boulder. I simply asked that you push on it."

When I first heard this story, I stood panting and dripping, looking back on the rugged, uphill trail our group had just climbed. I was four months into my first pregnancy, trying to keep pace with our fast and fiery teacher who tore up these rocky trails at alarming speeds and did not appear to believe in bathroom breaks.

Our group consisted of mostly college-aged athletes fifteen years younger than me, and in this rare moment of pausing to catch our breath, I looked around and thought, "What am I doing here? I should be nose-deep in a good book, not trekking ten miles a day in this impossible heat!"

I noticed the aches in my legs and back and thought of how I imagined spending my pregnancy with my feet up, finally allowing myself some rest. Instead, here I stood melting in the desert sun, breathing hot, dry air that felt like someone had aimed a blow dryer at my face. I wondered, "Lord, I know You brought me here. But why in the world must it be this hard and this hot?"

And now, years later, I can hardly believe I have returned to live in this desert. I find myself on that road, with my own shoulder pressing against an immovable rock. It is still difficult to be away from our family, our friends, and our home, and I do not yet understand why the Lord brought us here again. I believe this is His idea, but at the moment I cannot see a purpose in this strenuous road ahead.

The simplest of everyday tasks seem ridiculously difficult. My 10:30 A.M. class always wraps up later than its noon ending time, and so I have to run the uphill route to our apartment to feed Kate. It would be so much easier to let John give her a bottle and I could just stay on campus and grab lunch before my 1:00 P.M. class begins. But I know that if I don't nurse her midday, my milk will dry up. I am determined that she will have my best, even in this difficult place.

So I run the fifteen minutes back to our apartment, plop onto the couch, and nurse my sweet girl. Her eyes smile up at me, oblivious to my panting and dripping. Then I fly downhill back to campus, gulping the sandwich John made for me to eat on the way. I have many questions—"Lord, why have You asked this of me? Why have You brought us to Israel? Why must this be so difficult?"

But I am learning to walk and push by faith and not by sight. Things are not much easier since arriving a month ago, and it seems nothing has been changed by my efforts. Except that *I am changing*. When I press on as God asked me to, I cannot cling to the way I think things should be, or hold onto my own expectations of our time here.

I resented being powerless to move myself and my family past the initial, difficult time of adjustment, yet I am beginning to understand that powerlessness is the way to real strength. It brings genuine dependence and ultimately true intimacy with my Lord. I feel my arms, my back, and my legs are all getting stronger. I have found a surprising and deep peace in needing God this much and in embracing this dependence on Him.

I am learning to believe the words of James, "Consider it all joy, my brethren, when you encounter various trials, knowing that the testing of your faith produces endurance. And let endurance have its perfect result, so that you may be perfect and complete, lacking in nothing" (James 1:2–4).

And when the enemy whispers to me that nothing has changed, I feel the strength in my arms and legs, and notice the Lord's hand on my back, and I keep pushing. I am doing what God has asked of me, and simple obedience is changing me.

# Chapter 3

# Holes in the Text

When we look at this passage of the Text, we see a lot of problems with it . . ." Rabbi Moshe, our rabbinic literature teacher, went on to explain that the searching out of every nuance of every word and looking for "problems" in the Bible was the life work of *chazal*. These are the Jewish sages of old who preserved the legends, laws, and stories about Scripture.

The interpretations of the sages are known as the oral Torah, or classical rabbinic literature. This literature is considered by Jewish readers, students, and teachers of the Text to be the flesh on the bones of the written Torah (the first five books of Moses), which comprises the first section in the *Tanakh*, or Hebrew Bible.

The basic assumption of Jewish readers of the Bible is that the Holy One *intended* for the written Word to be rather incomplete, that is, for details to be missing. They believe the Author of the Torah meant for specific details of the people in the stories of the Bible to be talked about, and to be "fleshed out" by those hearing or reading them. Over centuries of time, *chazal* devoted their lives to this work, and as the missing details were created and interjected by trusted teachers of the Torah, they were eventually written down, thus becoming classical rabbinic literature.

This body of literature is voluminous, incredibly diverse, and filled with complex, creative, and even conflicting interpretations of the Text and its meanings. But to a Jewish mind, these conflicting interpretations are not a problem, because God's ways are big enough to be reflected in the many ways of interpreting the Bible. According to Rabbi Moshe, this literature is considered to be as holy as the Bible itself and is revered by its students as sacred text.

When I first heard Rabbi Moshe talk like this, I was offended. I view the Bible as a complete, finished work that cannot be added to or reduced. Who do these mere men think they are that their words are so holy? While they are assuming they can complete the Bible, I am assuming the thing to do is take something from it, and to bring to it only a willingness to learn.

However, as Rabbi Moshe continued to read and ask questions about passages of Scripture, and find "problems" and other such "holes" in the Text, I found myself drawn to this process of searching out the Scriptures and impressed by the imagination of the *chazal* and their view of God as being so infinitely complex.

I do not consider classical rabbinic literature to be holy, although I have found interacting with it deeply meaningful and exciting. I do not believe the Bible is incomplete without the interpretations of *chazal*, but thanks to studying in this manner I do find myself asking more questions of the Text and its Author than ever before. I am newly aware of three things, thanks to Moshe's good teaching.

To begin with, Jesus knew the rabbinic literature. There are instances recorded in the Gospels where Jesus quotes rabbis of old as He teaches the people. By speaking from the literature, the Master showed that He was very familiar with those sections in Scripture people wrestled with, and He gave them truth and answers they could live by. If He did this for people yet to trust Him as Messiah, how much more will He do this for us, His disciples? Jesus invites us to know Him in the Text!

The second thing Moshe contributed to my awareness in Bible study is that I have a great responsibility when studying Scripture. I believe the Bible to be as complete as God intended it to be, but now I see I can no longer read an obscure passage and say to myself, "Ok, that's weird," and move on. The Lord intends for us to read the Word with a genuine expectation that by God's Spirit we will know Him better in it. I believe the Spirit will equip me, because while I find the ways of the Holy Spirit to be infinitely mysterious, I trust Jesus' promise that, "the Holy Spirit, whom the Father will send in My name, He will teach you all things, and bring to your remembrance all that I said to you" (John 14:26).

And third, I have come to believe I am to search out the pages of Scripture with a passion greater than even the *chazal*. The Lord will equip me and even deepen my desire to acquire its wisdom and to apply it to my life. These are God's very words, and that would be enough. But more than this, I walk daily with the One who was the Word in flesh and is now the Word in Spirit. I believe that the Text is the Lord Himself, expressed in writing, waiting to interact with us, ready to teach us as we read.

As the words on the page speak into our struggles and our questions, it becomes the loving Person with whom we engage in the sacred, intimate, ongoing conversation that is as old as time.

# Chapter 4

# Shelter

One evening, they began popping up all around Jerusalem—the white linen walls and palm-branch roofs of *Sukkot* (pronounced *soo-khote*). You could sense the anticipation as families began constructing these temporary shelters on their balconies, in their small yards, wherever they had space.

Jewish people everywhere were about to spend a week eating their meals in these cozy little tents named in honor of the festival of the shelters, called *Sukkot,* or the Feast of Booths. God directly commanded the Israelites to keep this appointed time, to celebrate this holiday, as they entered the land of promise. He said it was His desire that the nation reflect on His goodness and provision during the forty years they struggled in the desert, living in temporary shelters.

John and I talked about how great it would be to have an invitation to eat a meal with a family in their shelter. We took evening walks each night of the holiday, admiring the various personal touches to people's *sukkot,* and the soft white light that illuminated the thin, linen walls. We could hear the families talking and laughing, and we wanted so much to join them. It was another sad reminder that we are foreigners here and of how hard it is to be outsiders.

I tried to make light of it, and said to John, "Of course we won't share a meal in a *sukkah* this year. How can we commemorate an experience in which we are still in the middle—struggling in the desert!" Yet when the holiday came to an end, I had to admit I felt we had missed something. We admitted to each other that it was hard to feel left out, and to miss out on such a beautiful and ancient tradition that nearly everyone around us was celebrating.

The week following *Sukkot*, John's parents flew in from Michigan to visit. We decided to have an early birthday party for Brynn, as she would be turning two later that month. We ordered a cake and invited the handful of people we felt blessed to be getting to know. There were fellow students, including our new babysitter Dawn, some neighbors, and friends from church. We kept it very simple, hanging a few balloons and streamers in a pretty corner of a nearby park, and serving cookies and cake from our favorite kosher bakery.

Half an hour into the party, I looked around at our new friends and thought, *These are such good people. Lord, you have given us such good people. They love you, Lord, and they love us and encourage us, and we didn't even know they existed two months ago!* Everyone was nibbling cookies and chatting happily. Brynn was completely engrossed in her new buddies on the playground, and baby Kate was napping soundly on her grandpa's shoulder.

I suddenly felt the Lord lean into me and whisper, *I am your shelter.* This caught me by surprise, but I felt those words ease into my heart with gentle warmth. For a moment, I just watched, basking in the joy of friendship and the newfound peace in my heart. It was an unforgettable moment of fully recognizing the Lord's hand on us.

He answered our prayers for sweet new friendships and even brought the reminder of the continued blessing of supportive, loving family. I have seldom been so aware of and so grateful for His presence. We may not have joined a Jewish family in one of the many beautiful *sukkot* we saw on those evening strolls, but the Lord has fully met us here in the in the desert, and He is indeed our shelter.

# Chapter 5

# Sanctuary: His Dwelling Place

In our studies here in Jerusalem, discussions often turn to the subject of the two temples that once stood in this city. They were each in their time the center of the universe for the Jewish people. We are learning to ask questions of the Text, so I wonder: Why would the God of Israel allow the destruction of His own dwelling place—twice? Was the second temple as holy as the first since it was built by Herod who did not follow God as did the first temple builder, Solomon. Why did the Holy One elaborate in such exquisite detail about the building of His temple?

The book of Exodus is commonly known as the account of the Israelites' divinely orchestrated escape from Egypt, but Dr. Barkay, our archaeology teacher, pointed out that it is mostly about the building of the temple. Given the elaborate blueprint, clearly God was serious about this structure.

For 480 years, intimacy with the Father came from the community maintaining purity and submitting to the spiritual authority of the leaders who were chosen from all the tribes by God. Then came the directive—build Me a house. Solomon, the king of Israel, was divinely appointed to oversee the project, and according to Scripture, all Israel assisted in this monumental task.

The Jewish people were devout in offering sacrifices to maintain a righteous standing before God—going to great lengths to attend the temple for the three sacred feasts, to offer appropriate sacrifices, and to be obedient to God in every way commanded. The priests, despite the literature's claims of their seasons of corruption, invested their lives to facilitate a complex system to intercede on behalf of the people of God.

Yet, the rabbis of old consistently warned the people not to turn their esteem of the temple into idolatry. They warned the people to obey God regarding festivals and sacrifices and to be careful not to shift their reverence from the Holy One to the temple and its rituals. Our teacher of rabbinic Judaism, Rabbi Moshe, called our attention to the Old Testament, the eighth chapter of the book of 1 Kings which records Solomon's dedication of the temple.

Solomon succeeded his father, David, on the throne of Israel, just as the Lord promised, and the temple is now completed in Solomon's reign. Amidst praises to God for faithfully keeping His promises, Solomon says, "I have built the temple for the Name of the Lord, the God of Israel. I have provided a place there for the ark (the presence of God)" (see 1 Kings 8:20–21).

"But will God indeed dwell on the earth? Behold, heaven and the highest heaven cannot contain You, how much less this house which I have built! Yet have regard to the prayer of Your servant and to his supplication, O Lord my God" (8:27–28). No one knew the awesome splendor in every square inch that building better than Solomon, yet he knew the structure itself was not worthy of reverence.

Our home congregation back in Michigan recently constructed a new building that is breathtaking. Much time and tithing were put toward an ambitious plan to give our community an attractive and spacious place to gather. Perhaps our objective was similar to that of the Jewish people who gave of their time and money to see the first temple completed. They wanted it to be the best-possible, earthly dwelling for God.

Some of our congregation think the expansion was influenced by the rapid growth of a nearby church, or maybe the mega-church movement in this country caught hold in our neck of the woods. In all the decisions made and money spent on color schemes, superior technology in sound and lighting, and seating capacity, many are wondering just who the new building is for.

Being away from our familiar place of worship has been hard for us. Certainly no church we have visited here compares in size, appearance, or technology. But, what we miss is not what we can see and touch, not tangible things. It is the heart of the people we miss. It is worshipping with dear friends, laughing, mourning, and studying the Scriptures in close community.

Surely there is more to our church than its hallways, coffee shop, and dozens of programs for all ages. Surely a church, if it truly is a group of Christ-followers, must be bigger than its walls. Like Solomon, let our prayer be that the Lord will bless the people who come and go from it. May we never make a building or even its best activities the focus of our affection. Let us say, "The heavens cannot contain You, much less this building we have built!"

Hear our prayers, Lord, as we join together in community to know You more and to passionately celebrate Your presence among us.

# Chapter 6

# Sanctuary:
# The Sabbath

I have still another question regarding chapters thirty-one and thirty-five of the book of Exodus. There we see instructions for building the temple, and, then—seemingly dropped in the midst of it—God commands the Sabbath. Why would God put those instructions on Sabbath observance here, amidst temple blueprints?

In my rabbinic thought class, we are learning to use new tools to read Scripture with probing questions. We are taught to consider the use of certain words and look for instances where the writer perhaps implied meaning simply by word choice.

For example, throughout Scripture the Hebrew word for *work* is *avoda* (pronounced *ah-voh-dah*). But in two places in the Text, a different word is used. The first is in the book of Genesis, where we read that God set about his work—here called *melacha* (pronounced *meh-lah-kha*). He created the universe and all that is in it, and when finished, the Creator rested from His *melacha*.

In Exodus, we see the second and only other use of that same Hebrew word for work. Here, the author conveys the Lord's instructions for the temple, and in chapters thirty-one and thirty-five, we follow a progression something like this:

instructions, details, REST from your *melacha*, more instructions, more details, and so on. Rather than using the word *avoda*, the common Hebrew word for work, the author used the word *melacha*.

Great rabbis ask two questions about these passages. First, why did Moses use this word choice for "work"? Second, why do we find this command to rest and observe Sabbath in the midst of all the instructions for the temple when most commandments are found together in another part of the Torah?

I pondered these questions as I made my way home from class. Why this special word for "work" in just these two places? Is God calling our attention to a parallel between the work He did in creation and the work of the Israelites in creating the temple? Is He drawing a parallel between his creation of a sanctuary for His people, and their creation of a sanctuary for God?

If so, then perhaps this provides an answer for the second question on why this command is in the midst of all the instructions for the temple. Just as God Himself rested from His creative work in making this world, our dwelling, we are to rest from our creative work in making His dwelling here on earth.

When this thought came to me, I literally stopped walking. I have always thought Sabbath was a good idea—that we should rest from the busy pace of life. But this idea implies that just as we give up household duties and workplace stress, we are to abstain also from our busy, though productive, religious activities (certainly building the temple was a worthwhile religious activity). If this commandment holds any meaning for us today, it means that one day each week we refrain even from busy church life. Heaven forbid (literally) anyone neglects rest by claiming to do "the Lord's work." Sabbath is very important to God.

Later, as I continued to make my way through Exodus, "important" became a gross understatement. In Exodus, chapter thirty-one, God says anyone who does not rest shall be put to death. Obviously, God was serious about this time of rest for His people. Yet, it was to be observed with joy and not treated as a yardstick of righteousness.

When Jesus walked the earth, He reproached religious leaders for their legalistic treatment of the Sabbath and their harsh words and penalties for people they believed to be violating it. However, we know the Son of Man kept Sabbath—He even calls Himself Lord of the Sabbath (Matthew 12:8). He simply kept it in a way that honored His Father—not men's rules. This sacred appointed time may look different for different people, but in light of His example, I believe we are to keep it. I am convinced that when we honor it, we honor Him.

In light of where the command is found, amidst blueprints for God's sanctuary, beloved Jewish author Abraham Heschel called Sabbath a "sanctuary in time." I love that. It is as though God built our sanctuary here on earth, created us to enjoy His presence in it, and rested. We construct His sanctuary on earth all week long as we continually build our lives and invite His presence, and then we are to rest as well, in His presence.

Rabbi Moshe teaches that, to the Jewish mind, the keeping of Sabbath is an acknowledgment that God—not us—made the world. In our loud and busy lives, we are to make a dwelling place to rest in Him, to dwell with Him—outside normal activity, normal time.

I feel the Lord beckoning to us, inviting us into this sanctuary in time. I know only a few Sabbath traditions, based mostly in rabbinic teaching, that faithful Jewish people have kept for thousands of years, and these seem a good place to begin. I wonder what will happen when we open our ears to the Lord of the Sabbath, accept His loving invitation, and invite His gracious instruction in how to personally and communally keep this day holy.

# Chapter 7

# Holy of Holies

After a long drive through the seemingly endless, barren, brown Negev desert, we saw from afar our first glimpses of the ancient city of Arad, seventeen miles south of Hebron. I imagined travelers in biblical times journeying by foot or on camel for days and, then, coming upon the formidable presence of these walls of Arad. We stood for a moment a few hundred yards away, marveling at its impressive acreage, the surprising height of its reconstructed three-thousand-year-old walls, and the massive thickness of its square watchtowers.

We approached the colossal gate and entered through it. Enemies came from the east, so to be ready to charge out in battle array, the gate of a city had to face east. This place was the work of Solomon, one of Israel's greatest kings. We know from Scripture that he fortified Arad as a stronghold in the south of the country putting Israel at a strategic crossroads to tap into a lucrative trade route used by the wealthiest nations of the world.

The Lord had a spiritual strategy here as well. He explained through Moses, as recorded in Deuteronomy, that He intended to put His people in a land where the greatest cultures of the world must come by and see for themselves the one, true God. By God's hand, David expanded the kingdom into the far reaches of this region of the world, and by God's sovereignty, Solomon further expanded the kingdom, and then fortified its boundaries.

Inside this walled city, there is a temple complex. We made our way to the partially reconstructed sacred space that had once been protected by a wall. Solomon built both the first Jerusalem temple and this one in Arad, so we can reasonably assume they were similar in layout. First, we noticed an altar rebuilt in more modern times in the very place the original stood. There was a long room with sockets for freestanding pillars, and at one end was a smaller enclosure built within the larger one.

A closer look at the archaeology of the site revealed exciting things. Indeed, the layout of the temple here was like the one Solomon built in Jerusalem. But Arad's temple was smaller, and we know that the Ark of the Covenant resided in the temple in Jerusalem, not here. Since the Ark of the Covenant was the presence of God, surely something symbolized His presence in this temple here in Arad.

Archaeologists found a standing stone at one end of this long room which was tucked into that smaller space. We know from Scripture that standing stones were erected by the people of Israel to mark a holy place—a sacred site where a significant interaction with the Holy One took place. All over the land of modern-day Israel and Jordan, such standing stones can be found, just as is described for us in the Bible.

We know the Lord told Joshua and the elders of Israel to stand stones taken from the Jordan River to commemorate the Lord's provision as they crossed into the land of promise. Joshua himself placed twelve standing stones in the river, so that anyone who asked why the stones were there would learn, "Because the waters of the Jordan were cut off before the ark of the covenant of the Lord; when it crossed the Jordan, the waters of the Jordan were cut off. So these stones shall become a memorial to the sons of Israel forever" (Joshua 4:7).

It seemed perfectly fitting to have erected a stone here because the Lord had provided a peaceful and powerful kingdom, and He further allowed Solomon to fortify this place. How fitting for it to be a memorial to the sons of Israel and to the world that there is a God in Israel.

But there is a problem. Archaeologists found two standing stones. Attempts have been made to reconcile this, but feebly. The two stones each had an incense-burning altar at its base, and they are clearly, intentionally standing within this smaller sacred enclosure. Written in both Hebrew and English, a short-posted, national park sign at the entrance to this enclosure read, "Holy of Holies." From other archaeological finds and conclusions drawn in temples in Israel and all over the ancient Near East, this most certainly meant that two deities were worshipped in this temple.

*Impossible,* I thought. How could a God-fearing king like Solomon, and his subjects, the chosen people of God, worship anything or anyone but the Lord alone? How could they have compromised their allegiance and their testimony in such a strategic place in view of the whole world for all those years?

Our teacher and guide, Dr. Wright, recalled biblical accounts of how some of Israel's kings followed God only, and some did not. Some built "high places" to other deities to appease the people embracing the culture around them. Scripture records that later in his reign, Solomon himself was guilty of this in Jerusalem, building high places and private temples to other gods on behalf of his many wives who worshipped false gods alongside, or instead of, the Holy One.

Scripture tells us that a handful of kings did what was right in the sight of the Lord and righteously tore these high places down. But, this isn't a private temple or shrine. This is a public temple in a major town on a major road, and it appears that the person responsible for its presence was the most powerful king of Israel's history. I wanted to chalk this whole thing up to a bad conclusion drawn by archaeologists and scholars. Certainly we must be careful what we assume from these archaeological finds.

But the case for two altars was building. Dr. Wright shared an inscription found on an incense burner in a similar, sacred enclosure excavated in a nearby ancient site, dated around the same time period. It said, "To Yahweh (the holiest name of God) and his Asherah." Our group fell silent.

An altar to the Holy One and to a Canaanite deity, who was the female goddess of fertility, was found at yet another major crossroads. I shook my head in disbelief. Who could have written such an inscription, and who could possibly have worshipped there?

After so much animated discussion about the towering walls of Arad, the well-maintained structure of the sacred enclosure, and the exciting testimony of the standing stone, our group was stunned and quiet. At last, we took a few pictures, commented quietly to one another, and dispersed to explore the site a bit more before lunch. I slowly walked on, pondering sadly what we had seen.

As I wandered the partially reassembled maze of ancient streets, a thought began to unfold in my mind. Scripture says that my life is a temple, and my heart the Holy of Holies, the place the Lord resides. *How many stones are standing in my heart? How many are standing in my life?* It may be easier to hide the standing stones in my heart; perhaps I can deceive myself about these idols and even veil them from others.

In my life, however, there are things that bear witness to my passions. The world sees these things and says, "Oh that defines her, that's what she loves." These idols are harder to hide, but it grows increasingly easy in our culture simply to justify them as socially acceptable vices.

Surely there are "high places" in my life, places the Lord hates to share. How do we guard our hearts, our lives, from the idols of this world? Left unchecked, these worldly idols could slowly leave their marked impressions on us, and we know they would eventually take up residence in our hearts.

Perhaps we must look honestly into each others' lives, deeply into each others' hearts. In community, we can celebrate the Lord's desire to be fully present there and, with the Lord's loving lead, we can embrace the process, however painful, of tearing down anything distracting us and the people in our lives from seeing the glory of God within us.

The Hebrew word *HaShem* means "The Name," and it is used as a substitute for "Yahweh," because this name for God is considered too holy to be pronounced. One archaeological scholar said it well: "There is *HaShem*, and all other deities—all made in our own image—the Canaanite gods. I'm done with the Canaanite gods."

# Chapter 8

# Yad Vashem

This week our class visited the Holocaust memorial in Jerusalem. It seemed out of place to me that after dozens of trips to various ancient sites, we would visit a museum commemorating an event from very recent history. But I was wrong. The intentionality of the Jewish people to commemorate even recent history raised important questions for us about the value of maintaining the past.

The name of the monument speaks volumes. *Yad Vashem* means 'a memorial and a name'. When Israel was declared an independent state in 1948, one of the first promises made by the Jewish nation was to give the victims lost in the Holocaust a memorial and a name. I was deeply moved by this tribute as I walked the halls honoring the million children who died and the families forced to hand over babies and the elderly to their occupying enemy. I greatly appreciated being given a glimpse into the lives of the brave survivors willing to tell the stories of those they lost and of their own miraculous rescues.

Walking among the displays of memorabilia left behind by the victims, including family photos, toys, and diaries, it truly seemed unthinkable such horrible atrocities could have been directed at any human being—let alone an entire people group. Whatever our political agendas or perspectives, no one can deny that the Jewish people have seen unfathomable persecution throughout their history. It seems vital to remember the victims, individually and as families and communities, and to honor their stolen lives and remarkable stories.

I was especially struck by the survival and continuity of the cultural and religious ideology of the Jewish people despite this time in history, yet another unwarranted era of their history of persecution. Outside of divine inspiration, how does a people group and their ideals maintain such a remarkable unity and vibrancy today?

Certainly there is value in a community's remembering, together, those we have lost in this world. I wondered, do we spend enough time honoring those who went before, recalling the beauty and even the hard lessons their lives hold for us? The biblical authors gave us stories of people's encounters with God, and often these stories included failures, loss, even death. But their relationships with God in the highs and lows of living, and what those encounters teach us about God's character, surely give us something to build our lives around in the modern world.

We will undoubtedly come across something in Scripture that isn't exactly clear to our modern-day minds. It is easy enough to set it aside as confusing and move on, or worse, repurpose it to suit an immediate need. Rather than search out the author's intent, we could leap to some false personal application, making what we want of the messages in the stories of Scripture.

Without good teachers and good community and the promised work of the Holy Spirit to reveal truth to us, we could easily miss some deeper value of the stories found in the biblical account, as well as the relevance of the work being done in our lives now.

When I think of our current culture, I do not readily see many ways we honor the past. Even our holidays, which were meant to honor the past, are instead spent honoring ourselves and reveling in the materialistic present. The word *replacement* comes to mind in thinking of our culture's view of the past. When we want something bigger or better, we replace the smaller with the bigger, or the older with the new. In some cases, this is necessary—like lost keys or a lost job. But maybe there are occasions we replace something, or someone, to attempt to fill a void that only time and hope can fill. Rather than truly deal with the grief of loss of someone we love, we search for an immediate distraction.

Perhaps we're too busy living for the future and all its perceived potential to reflect on the painful past. Whatever the reasons we may fail to remember the past, the enemy surely enjoys the advantage he gains when someone's story, its lessons, and the revealed nature of God in it go untold and are forgotten.

John and I have learned a great deal in our new lives here, so far. Mostly, we have learned that some of our previously held assumptions about biblical living were way off, and that some aspects of our lives are more reflective of our culture than of our God. We are grateful to be growing in our awareness that there is much the Lord wants to teach us so that we may live our lives as fully as He promises we will in Him.

# Chapter 9

# Reconstruction

early every class I attend at Jerusalem University College has the same objective, which is to reconstruct the past so we may more accurately read the biblical text. Without the work of history, archaeology, and ancient language study to reveal the world of the ancient Near East, we would know little about biblical context. Without world-class scholars (like the ones who stand before me in class), we could profoundly misinterpret the language and cultural imagery and the relevance of those words in Scripture's Old and New Testaments.

Everywhere you look here in Israel there are serious efforts to maintain the significant past. There are plaques commemorating important events, ancient ruins with their excavated treasures and unexcavated mysteries, and countless tombs, churches, mosques, and shrines maintained for their historical significance. Even the modern is historical. When I attended synagogue recently, I learned that every week Jews worship with liturgy that has been kept for centuries and is being used today in synagogues worldwide.

There is great significance in understanding and keeping the traditions of the past. The first followers of Christ were born into a culture and inherited a religion that was and still is determined to keep tradition, mostly according to the First or Old Testament. God established opportunities in numerous times and ways, ". . . that you may remember the Lord your God . . ." There is much to learn about how Christianity maintained and discarded certain traditions, how some ancient ways remain, and how some have been lost.

John and I talked at length when we got home from synagogue. One of the frightening realities we had to face when we decided to move to the Middle East was discussing who would raise our girls if some tragedy took us from them. We determined to never travel together on overnight field trips, and though it meant missing out on some valuable coursework and field study, we determined that at no time would both of us be across a border from the girls. We maintained these ground rules to minimize the time we would be away from them, but we knew that even our best and wisest intentions held no guarantees anywhere or at any time.

I thought again of our time at *Yad Vashem*. Heaven forbid we were taken from our children, I knew Brynn and Kate would be loved and well cared for by their appointed guardians. But I wondered in my heart, and finally out loud, "If something happened to us, who would tell the girls who we really were?" John put the same question better. "Who would *reconstruct* who we were so that the girls could somehow know us?"

Living outside the U.S. has caused us to appreciate a great deal about the freedoms and general Midwestern friendliness we took for granted. However, being away from the American way of life for a while has caused us to question some socially accepted norms that we hope to not embrace, let alone pass on to our kids. This is even true of some aspects of our Christian culture, and we want our lives and our girls' hearts, minds, and lives, to reflect Christ, not Christian culture.

We are shedding the false obligation to spend most of our time in church activity, especially activities that may be entertaining but do not build community. We are being freed from the socially esteemed busyness and overly full schedules that make us unavailable to the real needs of people around us. Instead, we feel called to be well within reach of our family, friends, and neighbors.

Most of all, we are compelled to walk away from the ridiculous task of juggling too many relationships that are not reflective of God's purpose for true community. We desire, instead, to build traditions and intimacy with loved ones so that together we build a great story of interacting with our God who made us and loves us abundantly.

My husband and I are taking a closer look at the biblical appointed times like Sabbath, and the seasonal feasts established in the First Testament and kept by Jesus and His followers in the New Testament. God said these were given so that regularly, weekly, seasonally, we would spend some time reflecting on how He has moved on behalf of His people in the past.

We are finding what countless generations of faithful observers already know—that these times of reflection lay a solid foundation of assurance that God has always been at work on behalf of those who love Him. Remembering God's history with His people is also building within us a trust He will provide for us today. We are even finding that time spent reflecting on the Lord's past goodness heightens our anticipation of His hand in what is to come.

# Chapter 10

# Faith Undone

"Jesus loved Martha and her sister and Lazarus. Yet, when he heard that Lazarus was sick, he stayed where he was two more days" (John 11:5–6). When I read this story in high school, I was so angry! I said, "Lord, why would You do that? They sent for You! They believed You could heal him, and You didn't go! Why would You not go and help them?"

I sat in a café in Bethlehem this morning, listening to my new friend, Dawn, tell her story. She has moved here to Israel permanently, certain the Lord wants her and a friend to open a guesthouse in Bethlehem and be a Christ-like presence of peace and prayer there. Despite the seasonal songs of its quaint tranquility and Christian history, Bethlehem is an unstable place frequently hostile to Christians. We decided to spend some time here so I could hear more about her journey.

Dawn told me more about her background. "I went to college, still struggling with depression, and my hypothyroidism just frustrated me. I kept saying, 'Lord, why won't You just heal this?' Lazarus' story was always in my head. The Bible even says some people were saying 'couldn't He who healed a blind man have kept Lazarus from dying?'

"What were his sisters and their friends thinking when Jesus finally walked into town? And when He asked Martha if she believed in Him, she definitely said yes. So, she proved her faith. She was obedient even when she must have thought Jesus failed her and her brother Lazarus. So Martha passed the test, so to speak, and now what?"

I thought to myself of all the ways I have been obedient in coming here to live and study in Jerusalem. I believed the Lord would take care of us, and I have called on Him continuously to meet our needs here. Yet after all these months, it is still not easy. I'm incredibly homesick for my regular routine and house and surroundings, and I constantly wonder if I am doing enough for John and the girls. Am I doing enough for my family and friends back home, while putting the time needed into my studies?

I believe I have the faith I am supposed to have, and I expected that by now I could be entering into an easier time. By God's grace, I often feel at home here in this place. But I want my friends and family back. Surely I have passed some test of obedience, yet I wonder when the Lord will show up and take care of these worries.

Dawn continued, "And then it gets worse. For about a year I felt like the Lord was tearing me apart, literally undoing me. In the Gospel of John, everyone involved knew Jesus could have healed Lazarus and didn't. Like me, they were probably wondering what He would have to say for Himself. And what does He say? 'I did this so the Son of Man would be glorified.'" And I thought, *well, that's great, Lord. Good for You. But meanwhile, Your family and friends have all been terribly hurt by something You could have prevented!*

Immediately I remembered having the very same thought over the past few weeks. My stepdad has had yet another stroke, and a new friend here just experienced her third miscarriage. I honestly cannot imagine why the Lord would not have prevented these hardships. These people love God, yet He lets them hurt. Why?

Dawn went on, "And then I was sitting in a seminary class, and I could hardly believe what I heard my professor say. 'It's just like the Lazarus story. He loved them too much to heal Lazarus. It was necessary that Lazarus die, because Jesus knew His friends had to be moved from *healing* faith to *resurrection* faith.'"

Resurrection faith. If we call ourselves Christians, this comes with a claim to resurrection faith. Yet I know I often demand healing on this side of the equation. I want help now. I want answers immediately. I call on God to keep me from pain or to help someone I love out of their hardship. I remind Him what He is capable of, and expect that He show divine power this way, or that. But as Dawn said, thankfully the Lord is too merciful to let us remain in that place of small expectations and too faithful to leave us the way we are.

I do believe Christ loves us too much to rescue us from the best part of His work—our obedience is just the beginning. Our obedience invites Him to turn us inside out, if necessary. It gives God permission to plow our hearts, preparing the good soil for the seed He intends to sow. It gives Him permission to move us past our limited expectations of simple and immediate solutions. And Lord knows He often must completely undo us to ready us for that move—that terrible, yet wonderful move from healing faith to resurrection faith. Then, and only then, can the real goal be realized—that in our lives, by His grace and unfailing love, He is glorified.

# Chapter 11

# Aqueducts in the Sand

ut when it came about that Ahab died, the king of Moab rebelled against the king of Israel. And King Jehoram went out of Samaria at the time and mustered all Israel" (2 Kings 3:5–6). Jehoram invited Jehoshaphat, king of Judah, to join him against Moab, and he agreed. Jehoshaphat asked his new ally, Jehoram, "Which way shall we go up?" Jehoram said, "The way of the wilderness of Edom."

I used to ignore this sort of passage in Scripture. I'd skim over the names of people, as well as, places. But I have stood in Edom, and I've seen the way of the wilderness that leads there. It is dry, barren, and difficult. It was dangerous then, and it is dangerous now. Jehoram and Jehoshaphat chose the most difficult route possible to go up against Moab. Why not the easier northern route?

"So the king of Israel went with the king of Judah and the king of Edom and they made a circuit of seven days' journey, and there was no water for the army or for the cattle that followed them" (2 Kings 3:9). No wonder it took them so long. Those armies could only march as fast as their slowest cow!

They had to bring their food with them, and now, they're out of water.

Jehoshaphat wisely suggested that Jehoram seek the counsel of the prophet accompanying them, Elisha. Elisha first responds to Jehoram by saying, "What do I have to do with you? Go to the prophets of your father and to the prophets of your mother" (2 Kings 3:13). Ouch. A pointed reminder that Jehoram's parents, Ahab and Jezebel, had turned their backs on God and worshipped the false god, Baal, the chief god of the surrounding peoples.

Jehoram asked again for help, and Elisha said that if not for the regard he had for Jehoshaphat, king of Judah, who did away with other gods in his land, he would not even look at the king of Israel!

Meanwhile, what are the soldiers thinking? They'd walked a week before even hitting the terrible desert. Another week later, they're out of water, and the one person who could help was holding a grudge against their king. It must have seemed totally hopeless. But Elisha eventually concedes to help, and when the hand of the Lord came upon him, he said, "Make this valley full of trenches."

Seriously? Build aqueducts in the desert? As if they hadn't spent enough energy getting here, now they're supposed to build aqueducts in the sand? These were not desert men. They didn't know the most common way to die out there in the desert was actually drowning. Walking along a dry riverbed, a person could suddenly be swept away by flash floods rushing down from the plentiful rainfall further north and east.

Elisha continued, "You shall not see wind nor shall you see rain; yet that valley will be filled with water, so that you shall drink, both you and your cattle and your beasts" (2 Kings 3:17).

Wouldn't it have been easier to just strike a rock and miraculously deliver a river? Or maybe while Elisha was speaking, a few rain drops could splash their faces? But no, the Lord had spoken, and they were to build aqueducts to catch rainfall they would not see.

Pondering this passage, I stood there at the site where these armies eventually faced the enemy at Moab. That seems like an awful lot to ask of people, especially tired and very thirsty men. Build an aqueduct and trust that rains are falling elsewhere to fill your trenches.

But is that really so much to ask? Aren't there many things in life we don't see or understand, but trust them to be there, to work? I have almost no comprehension of how my car engine operates, but do I look under the hood before I drive? I have mastered only high school physics, but I've never approached an airplane cockpit and said, "Hello, Mr. Pilot. I'd like to know just how this thing works before we take off today."

Surely I have plenty of proof of God's goodness in my life to know He is at work—even if it's beyond what I can see or understand.

> "It happened in the morning about the time of offering the sacrifice, that behold, water came by the way of Edom, and the country was filled with water."
>
> —2 Kings 3:20

I wondered, what if they hadn't built the trenches? What if they had considered the request too much to ask without any proof it was going work? That life-giving water would have reached them, and then they would have watched helplessly while it quickly seeped into the sand under their feet.

Living in the desert, I am learning to trust that even if I don't see the rain for months, the Lord is at work, sending rain elsewhere that eventually will flow our way. He says He will provide, and I am learning to believe Him.

# Chapter 12

# Mount Nebo

inally, here he stood.

He led a great number of people a great distance through danger, difficulties, and remarkable tests of obedience and faith in the Holy One. The people had rebelled and repeatedly rejected God and their own commitment to him made at Sinai. Despite moments of desperation and near loss of hope in the wilderness, here Moses and the Israelites finally stood.

The book of Deuteronomy tells the story of God bringing Moses and the Jewish nation to the land of promise. Deuteronomy is believed to be Moses' words as he stood at Mount Nebo and ushered Israel into a higher standard of faithful living than they had ever previously known.

Since bringing them out of slavery in Egypt, Moses claimed God had faithfully provided for every need. "To you it was shown that you might know the Lord, He is God, there is no other besides Him" (Deuteronomy 4:35).

Moses reminded them of the Lord's ever-present protection and said, "Know therefore today, and take it to your heart, that the Lord, He is God in heaven above and on the earth below; there is no other" (Deuteronomy 4:39).

Then Moses summoned all Israel and said to them, "Hear, O Israel, the statues and the ordinances which I am speaking today in your hearing, that you may learn them and observe them carefully."

The Ten Commandments. Rabbi Moshe said *commandments* is a decent translation, as the language can be reflected in the image of pulling a child aside and saying firmly, "I'll have a word with you." It connotes an authoritative expression of high expectations and a sharing of wisdom.

I've heard wisdom defined as, "skills for living." God's high expectation is total obedience with a motive of Fatherly love. This was a new code of covenantal, relational living from a loving God to the people He desired to bless with sweet harmony with one another and the utmost intimacy with Him.

Life in Egypt was a vague, distant memory, and nearly all of these people only knew the years of wandering in the desert. The Lord was preparing His people to enter a new place, a new kind of work, family, and community. To these people, crossing boundaries into new lands meant encountering new gods of foreign people. Certainly they wondered, "What does this place hold for us? Will our God be there?"

"Now Moses went up . . . to Mount Nebo . . . and the Lord showed him all the land . . ." Scholars believe it is impossible to see the entirety of the inheritance of the twelve Jewish tribes from this place. Some believe that the Lord supernaturally allowed Moses a view of the whole land from here, and others believe the passage is meant to be translated Moses *had seen* all the land. Walking from Egypt through Sinai, through modern day southern Israel and Jordan, northward to this lofty Mount Nebo, Moses had perhaps seen, even if from afar, each part of the land of promise. Yet he had never set a foot in it, and except for two men, neither had the people standing in front of him.

"Do *you* see all of the land of promise?" our teacher asked us as we stood in the sun, overlooking the Dead Sea from the modern day Jordan River. We could not. It was fairly hazy as the sun was setting over the Jordan. But we knew it was there. Unlike Moses, we had set foot in each of the territories designated to the twelve tribes. But the Lord was calling Moses and the people of Israel to a place they had never been and had never fully seen.

Moses recounts in Deuteronomy chapter thirty-one the many times the Lord went before the people and the many ways He protected them along their journey to this place. They were not empty-handed. They were armed on the journey with the new wisdom God gave them—called the Ten Commandments, and the promise of His presence going with them.

They couldn't see the land, but they had seen enough. They had seen the hand of the Lord on them, and they had experienced the Lord who went before them every step of the way.

I am learning it doesn't matter if we can see the road ahead. We have seen enough. We can rest assured that wherever God is taking us, He is already there. May we truly take heart in the counsel in Deuteronomy 31:6 to "be strong and courageous, do not be afraid or tremble at them [obstacles, enemies], for the Lord your God is the one who goes with you. He will not fail you or forsake you."

# Chapter 13

# Home Isn't

We have been home for a month now, but it doesn't feel like home. This last semester was a long six months. But shouldn't our house, our home of many years, feel more familiar? Since returning for the summer break, something has been off—way off.

We are surrounded by family and friends—weddings, barbeques, play groups. I now fill my days with everything I looked forward to in our last six month stretch of travel and studies in Jerusalem. My heart once craved to be here, yet most things about home now feel strangely unfamiliar. I feel guilty and a little annoyed when I acknowledge that *my heart does not feel at home.*

I tried to imagine how being home could fail to satisfy me. On a rare, quiet morning, I sat on my porch and looked back through my journal. I found a page from a few weeks ago when I was still reflecting on my trip to Jordan. I was wondering about the moment of truth, when the Israelites gathered on Mount Nebo. What were they feeling while standing at the edge of the land of promise? They only knew a culture where gods are territorial, and I believe they must have been wondering, "Will our God be there, in this unfamiliar place?" I sat on the porch, wondering, *Where is my God? The One who met my every need in the desert, who filled my breaking heart every time it cracked with loneliness and fear, and put me together until I felt at home in His presence in that foreign place . . .*

This place should be easy! I have no reason to feel lonely. I don't have to worry that war will break out on the street any minute, or that some angry religious extremist or politically-driven group will lash out near our school or neighborhood. I could hardly believe my own thoughts as I found myself wondering why the desert was *easier*.

This place is not easier as I expected, but forgetting Him here is. I forget to seek God's face, to crave and relish His presence in me and all around me. I forget to live in peaceful expectation that the Lord's hand is on my day. I forget to order my prayers the way I read in Psalm 5:3, "Hear my voice, Lord, at daybreak; in the morning I order my prayers before You, and eagerly watch." I forget to offer up my day to God and keep my eyes open to what has been planned for me. When things were very, very hard, I knew exactly where He was—in me, all around me. I can't miss God there, but I do a great job of ignoring Him here.

Here, I've taken matters into my own hands. I have filled the days with temporal, and tiring, activity. Worse, I realize sadly, I have done the unthinkable. Just like Israel coming into the land, just like the great King Solomon, I have bowed my heart to lesser gods.

Our summer break so far has been defined by countless hours sharing pictures and stories with curious acquaintances, making sure not to miss any invitations to gatherings and play dates before we head back, and running out to buy or eat what we can't get in Israel. I get up too late to look for God in the morning before the busyness begins, and our days are too full looking to be sure we have touched base with everyone to actually sit still and touch base with God. Rather than continue my new habit of quiet time with God in the morning, searching out Scripture throughout the day, and appreciating family time in the evening, I have fallen into my old ways. These ways were once normal for me, but they no longer fit.

People-pleasing, busyness, material distractions, and other gods have fooled me and failed me. The enemy would love for me to waste this precious summer, to turn it into a blur of forgettable activity, and to allow my inability to please everyone to steal my joy and gratitude that the Lord has brought us home for a time.

When I am still and look at our lives, I can hardly believe the incredible blessing all around us. We love our home. We relish quiet walks with our dog in the woods behind our house. We love slow evenings with a handful of people with whom we are building true community. The Lord wants us to spend every day enjoying His presence, as well as, loving and being loved by our family and friends.

I have missed starting my day with my Lord. And I am now grateful for how very disappointing these past few weeks have been, because it means I need Him that much, even when life appears easy. The really beautiful thing is that I think the Lord has missed me, too, and opened my eyes to realize my days are only worthwhile when fully focused on His presence.

Though this is home, it is different because I am different. In the desert, the Lord reshaped me and my desires. It was easy to see how the Lord prepared John and me for Israel by giving us great family, friends, and community to sustain us in our time there. But now I can see how He prepared us for Michigan, for home. In the desert, He stripped me of my lesser gods and let me know the sweetness of bowing my heart to only Him.

I expected to come home and not want to return to Jerusalem for our last semester. This is only partly true. Saying goodbye, again, will be hard. Leaving home, again, will hurt. But I must go back, because my Lord isn't finished with me quite yet. He is still teaching me that my heart is only at home when fully resting in Him.

# Chapter 14

# Sin Cycle

I sat on the deck of our apartment in Abu Tor, opened my Bible, and thought, *Please, Lord, don't let this just be homework.* I was feeling convicted by the woman who spoke in church today— our first Sabbath back in Jerusalem. She seemed to lock eyes with me and said, "Perhaps there is someone in this room who has made Bible study an academic pursuit. Don't forget your first love is Jesus." So I asked, *Lord, reveal Yourself to me in these pages.*

I opened Scripture to the book of Nehemiah. We are studying Nehemiah's mission to return from exile to rebuild the temple and the nation of Israel. Reading through chapter nine, I was moved by the heartfelt cry of the people begging for forgiveness. The leaders called the people to "stand up and praise the Lord your God!" (9:5).

I reread the chapter, taking note of the cycle: You (God) chose us (the people of Israel). We failed You, You rescued us, gave us the Law, then, we failed You again. We repented; You saved us again and blessed us enormously. We rebelled again, we cried out again, You saved us again, and we find ourselves again in bondage. We beg You in all Your goodness to "not let this hardship seem trifling in Your eyes" (9:32).

I found some things intriguing in this passage of Scripture. First, the unity. The people saw each other's sin as their own, even the sins of past generations. They knew that personal sin is not only personal, but that it affects the whole community. They fully understood that sin's reach is deep and wide.

The second thing I found intriguing was the humility. They simply confessed "we have fallen short, despite the clarity of Your Word to us." I recalled someone telling me that true confession is seeing our sin the way God sees it. Excuses are easy, but God's Word is clear. We must address our sins specifically, in community, and daily acknowledge our need for Him.

And third, I found their sheer honesty intriguing. I also worry that my hardships seem trifling to Him, and that one of these days I just might get something of a grace overdraft notice. Perhaps we avoid God when we are most in need of mercy. We might call it a lack of self-confidence, but what if it truly reveals a lack of confidence in *Him*? Do I really trust the heavenly Father to "consider our groaning," as penned in the Psalms, and save us when we ask?

I thought back to another class session when Rabbi Moshe referenced the first two chapters of Hosea in light of Israel's sin cycle. *Adultery* is the name God gives the sin of walking away from Him to go one's own way. Every time we walk away, it is to chase false gods like materialism, lust, social gain, or personal comfort. Deuteronomy states that God's penalty for adultery is stoning to death.

Yet in Hosea 2:23, God forgives His wayward people. He says, "I will call you My people and you will know Me." Rabbi Moshe posed the question, "Will God set aside His own law so we can know Him?"

I had never thought of forgiveness that way. It seems the Lord forgave His people over and over, finally providing perfect atonement in Christ's sacrifice to show His great love for His creation. If I ever doubt the vastness of divine mercy and need a reminder of God's abundant loving-kindness, I will run straight to the book of Hosea.

In my desire to see the Messiah in this passage, I wondered what Jesus said about repeated sin. I searched out the opening books of the New Testament. On His way to Galilee, Jesus passed through Samaria where He met a Samaritan woman at midday at the town's well (John 4:7–30). She likely drew water in the heat of the day to avoid the scorn of her neighbors who all knew her sordid past. Jesus knew she had failed repeatedly to honor God by living with various men, married to none of them, and He revealed to her His knowledge of her sin. Jesus was kind, loving, and He set her free.

Jesus broke all sorts of social and religious rules even to speak to an unclean person, a Samaritan, and a woman. John records that she and her community repented and were saved, and she wasn't even looking for Him.

When Jesus taught the disciples how to pray (Luke 11), He directed them to regularly ask for forgiveness. He recognized our constant need for it, and then tells a parable about a persistent friend who gets what he needs simply because he is insistent— implying that if a friend will do this for another friend, how much more will your loving Father do this for you?

Peter asked, "Lord, how often shall my brother sin against me and I forgive him? Up to seven times?" (Matthew 18:21). Rabbis of the day said to forgive three offenses, so Peter probably thought he was being really generous in saying seven. How did Jesus respond? "I do not say to you, up to seven times, but up to seventy times seven" (18:22). It doesn't matter what the world around us says is generous or gracious, because God's heart is always more generous and abundantly gracious.

And when an adulterous woman was brought before Him by a self-righteous crowd of accusers, Jesus simply said, "If any of you is without sin, let him be the first to throw a stone at her" (John 8:7). He stooped down and with his finger wrote on the ground as the crowd dispersed. Then, He told her to go and repent.

Some details in this passage remains a mystery. Did the scribes and Pharisees scatter because of what Jesus wrote on the ground? If so, what could He have penned in the sand that sent her unforgiving accusers away? I imagine the Lord writing Scripture, perhaps from Hosea. Maybe His words referenced a passage serving as a reminder of God's limitless grace, the sort of grace meant to be reflected in our relationships with one another.

This encounter was meant to test Jesus to develop grounds for accusing Him. They wanted to see if this teacher would fall into line, upholding the laws as interpreted by the religious teachers of the day. Jesus once again astonished the crowd, and once again, abundant mercy is the rule.

If anyone had the right to be indignant in the face of habitual sin, it would be the Man who would die for it. Yet He responded in accordance with His Father's heart, with passionate love and complete forgiveness.

Whatever the world's standards would lead us to believe about what we do or do not deserve, we can take heart. He has overcome the world. Like the rescued and redeemed disciple named Paul, I look at all I know of the God of the Bible and the life and work of Christ, and "I am convinced that neither death, nor life, nor angels, nor principalities, nor things present, nor things to come, nor powers, nor height, nor depth, nor any other created thing, shall be able to separate us from the love of God, which is in Christ Jesus our Lord" (Romans 8:38).

# Chapter 15

# Who Do You Say That I Am?

Walking the road to Caesarea Philippi from the Sea of Galilee gave us plenty of time to ponder Jesus' journeys in these same places. While the truths, wisdom, and hope in the teaching of Jesus are timeless, we are learning to see they are also distinctly rooted in the time and place where the Master walked and taught.

The more we explored the historicity of Jesus' life, the more we could see the application of His words to His immediate audience. For example, when the Lord approached the Samaritan woman at the well, it was for her rescue, redemption, and restoration. The Samaritans were considered to be outside the blessings of God, and women of ill-repute were typically shunned, especially by rabbis. By this story we can know that despite who we are in the world's eyes, Jesus will find us and restore us. He associated with the untouchables of society, and He put His hand of redemption on lepers, prostitutes, and dishonest businessmen. We can rest assured that none are outside His reach.

In the sixteenth chapter of the Gospel of Matthew and the eighth chapter of the Gospel of Mark, Jesus took His disciples two days' journey north, from the provincial security of their religious communities to the region of Caesarea Philippi. Surely as they approached this place, they grew nervous, apprehensive, and wildly uncomfortable with where this was leading. They knew what went on here. Jews in that day believed Caesarea Philippi to be the filthiest, most perverse place on earth. The pagan worship of the goat god and related sexual revelry were so vile that rabbis claimed the Messiah could not come to the earth while Caesarea Philippi stood.

Archaeologists have uncovered a temple there dedicated to the god Pan, acclaimed by his followers to be the "Son of God." The entire temple complex, fully active in Jesus' day, was built into an enormous rock face and was adjacent to a cave with a stream flowing from it and considered by the people to be the very gates of hades (hell).

Yet here Jesus came, nervous young disciples in tow. He paused and pointedly asked of them, "Who do you say that I am?" Peter answered, "You are the Christ, Son of the living God." Jesus affirms Peter's answer, and then says, "On this rock I will build my church, and the gates of Hades will not overcome it" (Matthew 16:18).

I am learning that when I first ask what Jesus' listeners heard, I can better conclude what I am to understand in His words. Certainly they heard His promise that the gates of hades will not stand. No matter what other rabbis said, here stood their long-awaited Messiah before them, promising that even the most foul human failings could do nothing to hinder the Kingdom coming.

Yet I wonder, what *rock* does Jesus mean? Peter, in his leadership role in the early church? Many branches of Christianity embrace this interpretation. But here the word *rock* is feminine in its original Greek. Did Jesus mean the truth itself that Peter stated—that Jesus is Messiah, the one and only Son of God—is the rock?

The Greek word *petra* is best translated as simply the common word for "rock." I have heard the suggestion that perhaps Jesus was referring to that very rock face they were looking upon. That tall face of rock hosting the lost of the lost, the people worshipping everything but the one, true God? Could Jesus have been saying that upon this rock, upon people just like this—very lost, very disillusioned people—I will build My church?

Not a very safe idea, entrusting the kingdom to unfit, unworthy people.

By now, the disciples have seen Jesus take the kingdom to places they likely hoped to avoid. He healed a demoniac living in tombs within a day's walk of three anti-Jewish, pagan cities. He miraculously fed the multitudes of some of these towns. He healed a Syro-Phoenician girl, and even healed a Roman centurion's daughter—an offspring of an officer of the enemy and occupier of Israel.

Surely the disciples were marveling that their Jewish Messiah brought the kingdom of God to those peoples whom other rabbis judged and shunned, casting them out in the name of God. What was Jesus teaching them about who is lost, and who can be found?

I thought about what I saw a few years ago in Turkey, formerly Asia Minor of the biblical account. I recalled that for the young men who walked with Jesus daily, this trip to Caesarea Philippi was just the beginning. They would be called to bring the kingdom of life and hope to spiritually, culturally, and even physically unsafe places.

What a dangerous thing the Lord called them to do.

Yet by their obedience and His Spirit, those young disciples told their testimonies to all who would hear, and the world was changed. These stories, the writings of the New Testament, still change lives today.

If we call ourselves followers of Jesus, is he expecting any less of us? What is the Messiah we sing about, pray to, and acknowledge as our salvation preparing us for? If His love is the model—and He says it is—no one is outside the reach of the Lord, and no one is beyond the hope of the Father's love. It seems that walking with Jesus, truly getting to know Him, is the only way to learn who we are, and who God is asking us to be.

# Chapter 16

# Making Jesus

I have just completed a course called The Life of Jesus. I am humbled and excited by how much I have yet to understand about Jesus, His lifestyle and culture, and those who opposed Him. The more I learn about the Lord in books and church, the more questions I have.

I am so grateful the gospel writers wrote their accounts of life with Jesus, and I am grateful for the Scriptures as a place to go with my many questions. With guidance from the Holy Spirit, the writers of the gospel accounts wrote to the churches they led, their neighbors, even their own families. These were men in ministry, walking with people and wrestling with tough questions, dealing with difficult life issues. They wrote to convey the deeply personal love and redemption they experienced walking with the Messiah, the Son of the living God.

In their time with Him, the disciples were also struggling to know better who Jesus was. Perhaps many of the greatest moments revealing His nature and character came in His interaction with both friends and enemies.

In Jesus' day, many devout Jews called Pharisees wanted this popular teacher to fall in line with them, and they argued endlessly with Him over religious issues. Scholars believe Jesus interacted more with the Pharisees than other religious parties because, being teachers of the Torah, they had much in common.

But Jesus was different, and this frustrated and often infuriated the Pharisees. He refused to put men's law above God's, and insisted the kingdom of God is about obedience as the result of love (Matthew12; Luke 13, 23), not because of duty. He did not match their expectations of what the Messiah would be, and, unable to see beyond their own agendas, they did not recognize Him.

The Zealots wanted Jesus to take up arms with them, to stir the people to overthrow Rome and take back the land. The Zealots were ready to rid the temple of its corrupt leadership and to reinstate true priestly leadership over a sovereign state. Some scholars propose that Judas, who was a disciple and a zealot, betrayed Jesus in his impatience for Jesus to act on a military level. Perhaps he thought the time for teaching and talking was past, and it was time to act and usher in the Kingdom. Having Jesus arrested would force His hand and, surely, then, if Jesus was truly the Jewish Messiah the Zealots expected, He would call for war against Rome.

But when Jesus taught that the kingdom of God is about love and forgiveness for all, even Gentiles, and when He entered Jerusalem riding on a donkey (a sign of peace), many rejected Him because He was not a politically rebellious Messiah. In fact, Jesus remained nearly silent about Rome's rule of the land, and thus the Zealots found this position intolerable, and they could not accept Him.

The temple authorities, the religious rulers of the Jews, were called Sadducees. They did not seem to care who Jesus was until He became impossible to ignore. They enjoyed an easy life, benefiting from both the pious keepers of Judaism, whose temple sacrifices gave them a nice income, and the occupying

Roman authority, who introduced them to the worldly pleasures of Greek culture.

We know of only two Sadducees who interacted personally with Jesus prior to His trial: a ruling class Pharisee named Nicodemus and a man named Joseph of Arimathea. In the third chapter of John we read that Nicodemus approached Jesus with real personal interest. In John chapter seven, we see Nicodemus calling for legal justice on behalf of the arrested and accused Jesus. Joseph of Arimathea gave up his personal tomb, a very expensive gesture, so Jesus' body could be laid to rest in it. These men actually recovered Jesus' crucified body from Pilate and helped bury Him. Matthew chapter twenty-seven even claims Joseph was a disciple of Christ.

Outside of these men, however, we know the Sadducees did all they could in their power to see Jesus silenced, and when they came to the limits of their own authority, they appealed to Rome to have Jesus crucified. When Jesus taught that the kingdom of God is about personal and community purity, higher moral standards, and that loving people outweighs even temple activity, the Sadducees simply could not tolerate Him.

We know there was much opposition to Jesus in the time and place into which He came, just as there is much opposition to Him today.

There are religious teachers and leaders with self-serving agendas, some more concerned that they are heard and revered than that Jesus is known.

There are politically-motivated Christians who spend more time and resources lobbying government than loving their neighbors, more concerned with building a Christian political nation than building the kingdom of God.

And there are people who simply want to ignore Christ for the sake of living life as they please, choosing to be free from their Maker.

Jesus does not promise comfort or ease in this life, not even when we follow Him, and so even today many simply refuse to embrace Him.

But what did the Lord promise? And what do we believe about Him? What have believers made of Him in their lives? I know that whatever we think of Him now, there's more to know. Whatever we believe about Him, there's more to understand. Whatever measure of faith we claim, He has immeasurably more to show us.

May we pour these New Testament stories about Jesus into our hearts and minds and better know His vibrant presence, kind sense of humor, inexhaustible compassion for the hurting, and His healing touch. And as we get to know Jesus as revealed by those who walked with Him during His life on earth, may others see the Savior through those of us He is redeeming today.

# Chapter 17

# Having Nothing, Lacking Nothing

When I stood here for the first time a year and a half ago, I was exhausted, grieving, and shaken to my core. John had been away for a few days on field studies, and he would be gone a few more. I was so homesick, constantly worried about our safety, and lonelier than I had ever been. The girls, then babies, were not sleeping well and were terribly unsettled.

Then we received the phone call that a couple very dear to us, our best friend's parents, were killed in a bewildering plane crash. How could we bear one more hardship? How could we possibly comfort our friends and mourn fully from Israel? Were we supposed to repeat the impossibly long journey back across the world, dragging our babies back across sleep-depriving time zones?

Despite the dark fog of shock and fatigue that lay heavy in my head and heart, I had somehow put the sleepy, sweaty girls into the stroller and set out to attend service at a church. I hadn't been to this particular church yet, and I was in no mood to worship or to meet new people. Still, something had pulled us out the door and across town to Narkis Street. I remember that first walk to church, forty-five minutes entirely uphill in the blistering sun.

As I pushed the double stroller up the uneven sidewalks, I recall checking and rechecking my map. Was it really this far? I noticed the stroller sagging to one side, and groaned out loud—our fifth flat tire in three days. I have to wonder if I would have ever visited that church had I known how far it was and how difficult the walk would be.

Looking back, that question was fitting. Would I have even come to Jerusalem if I had known how hard it would be? Finally we arrived, and I picked both girls up out of the stroller and took a place on the aisle. I remember standing, rocking hungry Kate with an eye on Brynn nibbling crackers next to me in our row of folding chairs. Sweat streamed down my back as I panted, trying to catch my breath while scanning the back of the room for a place to nurse Kate. How could I bear this? Everything about living here so far was just too hard, too hot, and too tiring. *Really, Lord? This is what You have for us here in Jerusalem? How can I stand this?*

There was a pause in the service, a moment of quiet rustling, and then a woman's voice began singing,

*"Here in the power of Christ I stand . . ."*

I was suddenly only aware of those words, and I could hardly believe my ears. As that sweet, clear voice sang on, the fog seemed to dissipate a bit and slowly lift off of me, and so did the desperate loneliness, helplessness, and fatigue. Here was the answer to my heart's longing—a safe and sure place to stand.

Hot tears spilled onto my cheeks, and a few moments later, I quietly sang along. Healing began. The girls seemed moved, too. Kate stopped squirming and played contentedly with her fingers, and Brynn stood in front of her chair smiling and swaying with the music. I can still recall the sense of peace and calm that came over me, and I knew I was right where I was supposed to be.

I remember that within the hour, kind women were taking turns holding the girls. When we broke into groups of four, strangers prayed with me for our settling in, and for peace in the loss of our friends. When I was finally in a place of having nothing, I was ready to receive everything the Lord had for me.

This morning I stood in the same row of folding chairs in our dear little church, with John beside me and the girls sitting with their friends. Most of our field studies were complete, we were hardly apart from each other anymore, and we had our sights set on final exams and exit projects. We would soon be returning home for good, and this was the last Sabbath service we would attend. I looked around, mentally capturing every detail of the place. I wanted to remember this cozy room, these friendly faces.

Imagine my surprise and delight when the worship team paused and began singing that very song,

*"Here in the power of Christ I stand . . ."*

My heart leapt, and I was overcome with gratitude as I realized how much had changed since our first attendance. It has passed so quickly, yet strangely, that time seemed to hold the trials, adventures, and joys of an entire lifetime. So much has changed. We certainly have.

I looked around and newly appreciated the comfort of familiarity—our friends Joanne and Quincy leading worship, Martha and a few of her five kids sharing snacks with the girls, people holding or chasing their kids, and the still odd but now familiar sight of Franklin walking around the sanctuary looking to throw in a few notes on his trumpet.

Along with the familiar, we have grown to appreciate the rather unstructured and spontaneous nature of the Sabbath morning together. The few consistent elements we can anticipate are welcoming the dozen or so visitors representing at least half a dozen countries, the hearing of God's Word in our weekly Torah reading, and numerous opportunities for people to share their concerns and praises publicly.

I am so grateful for the sweet fellowship here, and for the inviting warmth of the regulars toward newcomers in this loving, diverse community. While it seemed oddly chaotic in the beginning, I have come to appreciate the spontaneity of the pastor and worship leaders to allow people to share as the Spirit leads regardless of how scrambled the morning service ends up looking. The Lord led us to this place where we are fully embraced as family, showing us the beauty of authentic Christian community.

This morning we read from Deuteronomy chapter thirty-two. God spoke to the people of Israel before bringing them into the land of promise, foretelling their failures, and promising His unwavering provision. He reminded them they would arrive at the land as completely aware of their need for Him as when He sustained them in the desert.

But on Mount Nebo, the Lord had warned the sons of Israel that as they entered the land and it yielded its bounty to them, they would slowly forget God and their need for Him. God said He would allow a time of oppression and difficulty, and then, when the people again could fully acknowledge their need, He would restore them.

I am being restored. This morning as those words from Deuteronomy were read, I felt the Lord stir in my heart, and I realized that the story of the people of Israel was my story as well. I have become too comfortable in my assumptions, and some of my ideas have kept me far from Him. I had too much to realize what I truly needed, which was more of Him.

How precious the realization that God loves me too much to allow me to reach the place He is leading me to without first teaching me how to truly live there.

# Chapter 18

# If Anyone Is Thirsty

It was *Simchat Torah*, called the last and greatest day of the Feast of *Sukkot*. For the past week, the people of Israel and Jews throughout the world celebrated by building *sukkot*, or small tents, on their patios or yards. Many ate every meal there to remember God's provision for the Israelites when they lived in tents in the desert. Some even spent whole nights in the tents.

This year was very different from last year for a number of reasons. First, we were invited to join a family in their *sukkah*. Last year we had wanted so desperately to be invited into one of these cozy, warmly lit tents. This year, our neighbors asked us to join them for mid-morning tea and cookies. We loved taking part in such an ancient tradition and feeling more part of the community here.

Also, we spent *Sukkot* anticipating a third child! We found out earlier this month that I was pregnant. We could barely contain our joy at the idea of heading home in a few weeks and taking this new life with us. We were eager to tell our family and friends, who had mourned a miscarriage with us only a few months ago. What joy we could all share in this new hope!

Despite our anticipation, we decided to wait until we could tell them in person, at home. We most looked forward to telling our little girls because we knew they would be thrilled about having a new baby in the house.

But the last and greatest day of the feast became the darkest day I can remember. In the afternoon, I began bleeding. All day I watched and waited, agonizing as time passed and the bleeding did not stop. I cried and pleaded, *Lord, please fix this! I don't want to lose this baby!*

Despite my tears and hours of begging, by morning it was clear we had lost the child I carried. I was terribly shaken, being this far from the comfort of home in Michigan, my midwife, and my family. Sadness overwhelmed me and I just could not stop crying.

Then I got angry. *We haven't dealt with enough struggles here? How could You let this happen? Lord, this is Your best for us?*

The thought pressed on my heart, *This is not My best.* For a time, I ignored it, knowing it was the Lord and I was too angry to hear it. But eventually, I listened. *This is not My best.* But aren't we promised His best? Everything we experience passes through His hand, right? That's what I have always believed.

But in that dark time of such fear and hopelessness, I began to question the things I have always believed. I thought about life's worst, the experiences that really break us and tear our hearts and lives apart, things like death, loss, and miscarriage. These cannot be God's best.

My friend Cathy came over. We recalled the joy we both felt last week when we were sitting together in a coffee shop and I burst out, "I'm pregnant! I can't keep it secret anymore! We haven't even told our parents yet, but I'm bursting!"

"I wouldn't trade that joy for anything," I said quietly. She looked into my face and said, "Melanie, the Lord will redeem this." The words poured into my parched spirit like sweet, refreshing water. I knew in every inch of me that it was true. It's what the Lord does. He redeems pain, brokenness, and tragedy. I can find no promises in Scripture that God will prevent all of our pain, but everywhere are the promises and proofs that He can and will redeem it.

I thought of the Israelites in the desert. Desperate for food, water, and safety, they cried out to the Lord. Despite their cries and terrible suffering, they were not taken out of the desert. Instead, God provided food, water, and safety for them in the place He brought them, in that desert. More importantly, He shaped them into a people fully aware of His goodness and mercy. His provision, His shelter, His redemption. These are His best.

In the seventh chapter of the Gospel of John it is recorded that Jesus celebrated *Sukkot* in Jerusalem. On the last and greatest day of the feast, the hundreds of thousands of people gathered fell silent as the priest poured fresh water onto the altar, the drink offering. They had been drinking muddy cistern water for months and were desperate for the autumn rains. This drink offering was like saying, *Lord, this is it. This is all the water we have left. We will pour it out to You because we believe You will save us!*

We know what Jesus had to say about thirst. Perhaps it was in the silence of that moment that the Lord stood and shouted, "If anyone is thirsty, let him come to me and drink" (John 7:37).

Lord, I am so thirsty, and I desperately want to feel safe and whole again. I hate this desert and I want out. Any hope left in me, I pour out to You, and I beg You to save me.

# Chapter 19

# The Best Is Yet

For the past couple of days, as we prepare to leave Jerusalem for good, my neighbor Ruth finds excuses to stop over. Usually it is to drop off something she knows the girls loved playing with and she thinks we should take home to Michigan. She says her grandkids have outgrown it anyway.

We have spent so many precious evenings together across the hall in her living room. We enjoyed hours looking at family slides, eating cookies, celebrating birthdays, and playing with the finger puppets which now live permanently behind her couch's pillows.

I remember the first time she knocked on my door. "Is that tall husband of yours home? I need a pair of strong arms, if he doesn't mind."

I said, no, I'm sorry, he's away. But can I help?

She waved her hands, "No, no . . .", backing out of my doorway. But I followed her across the hall anyway. Frank had fallen in the bathroom and needed help getting up. He has heroically battled Parkinson's for over twenty years, and some days are harder than others.

Ruth and I managed to lift him to his chair, and then she shooed me away, grateful but not wanting to impose. But we often imposed. Most nights after the girls' baths, they scampered over in their pajamas to say goodnight to Mrs. Ruth and Mr. Frank. They would hold his still, cramped hand, cover his lap with toys and dolls and books, and sometimes climb right into his wheelchair with him. Ruth and Frank became our much needed family away from home. I think she is almost as sad about the coming quiet across the hall as we are about leaving her and Frank.

More recently, she has been giving us books from her vast library. It's time to get rid of some of this clutter anyway, she says. I have to chuckle inside when she gives us books written in Hebrew. She has more confidence in our newly acquired Hebrew skills than she should.

It was the day following our miscarriage, the day after *Simchat Torah* that ushered out the Feast of *Sukkot*. Ruth stopped by with a book about the Jewish feasts. She explained that all good Jewish homes have this book in their collection, and it is a wonderful guide to appreciating the traditions of the various festivals. She had earmarked some of her favorite pages, and spent a few minutes pointing out what they said about *Sukkot*, about Sabbath, and even *Purim*, a Jewish cultural holiday celebrating the events recorded in the book of Esther.

As soon as Ruth left, I sat down and looked for the page on *Simchat Torah*, called the last and greatest day of the Feast. I have come to realize that the Lord has great purpose in these appointed times, and I wanted to know what the book said about this day that is forever marked in my life as the day I lost my baby. The author said that on this last day of the feast, when people take down the walls of their tents, they pray they never build another.

How odd, I thought. The Jewish people love this holiday, and they spend weeks in preparation for it. Why would they pray that they never have another? I read on. At the end of the feast, they pray that they never see another Feast of *Sukkot*! "May Messiah come and dwell with us, and we need never build another *sukkah*," they pray.

"What a prayer," I whispered. What a remarkable idea, to live in such anticipation of the Lord's return that we pray to abandon even the best of this world for it.

I had grown up with the truth of Messiah's coming all my life and I know that Jesus will return. But somehow I had simply set this promise aside as mysterious and distant.

Now I was ready to really embrace it. In my heart's desperate groping for something to hold fast, I found it there. I felt the Lord standing before me with His hands out, inviting me to surrender the worst kind of pain this world can bring for the hope of His coming. The Lord will redeem this.

Lord, may that day come soon. May we soon cease to experience the worst of this fallen world, and may we not allow even the best of this life to distract us from the unmatchable hope of the glory of that day that is to come.

# Chapter 20

# Leaving the Desert

*What stays . . . anything we have outgrown . . . tiny pink clothes, baby bibs . . . what goes home . . . the girls' favorite toys and our favorite books.*

I am finding packing to be more of a challenge than expected. I have dreamed of the day I would leave Jerusalem and return home to Michigan, and now that it is time, I am surprisingly torn. It's easy to determine what fits in our luggage, but hard to prepare to say good-bye to this place.

The Lord has greatly blessed our marriage here. Having only each other for a time and sharing the adventures of figuring out life in this place have grown our friendship enormously. John made the most of his precious daddy-daughter time when I was away or studying, and despite our rigorous schedule, I do not feel I missed a moment of the delightful growth of our girls.

John and I have been honored to attend Jerusalem University College alongside some dear, new friends, and studying under some of the greatest minds in the fields of biblical archaeology, historical geography, and ancient Near Eastern history. We are immensely grateful for the dedication of our school's director and his wife to keep the school functioning despite the political unrest that frequently stirs.

Best of all, studying with John has been a true partnership, encouraging one another's focus and diligence. We anticipate years of unpacking and sharing the knowledge entrusted to us with each other and whoever desires to learn alongside us.

Our little church on Narkis Street was a sanctuary for our souls, as Jesus truly met us in the good people there. The fellowship and sharing of Scripture was always worth the long, uphill journey.

Our beloved friend, Dawn, has been a precious gift to our family, and in her care of Brynn and Kate, she is the reason I could invest so much time to study. Besides loving and praying over us, the Lord had yet another purpose for her in our lives: she has opened our eyes to the movement of the Lord in Bethlehem, her new home.

We cherish the friendships found in Ruth and Frank across the hall, the Kramers up the street, and even Claude and his wife, Simone, who run the little French patisserie around the corner. Claude always knows what I will order and says with his charming French accent, "I have but one customer, and her name is Melanie." What a delight.

The beauty, diversity, and history of this land have deeply moved us, and compel us to return to spend yet more time discovering its endless natural and historical treasures. We have been captured by the wildly beautiful desert as well as the lush springs and forests of the northern hills and valleys. We pray the Lord has plans for us to return to this awe-inspiring place.

It is most difficult to leave behind the simplest parts of our regular routines, such as times in the park with Kate and bakery dates with Brynn. We have raised our girls in this little apartment, and by now they have lived more in Jerusalem than in Michigan. There are elements of our lifestyle here that I am surprised I prefer. For example, having no car and walking everywhere has kept us fit, and the strange but healthier food, and the quiet life of graduate work have both been wonderfully nourishing.

Instead of being "annoying city noise," hearing our neighbors going about their day has become reassuring—especially when John was away for days on field studies. I thought I would never be able to sleep hearing voices below and above us, but I have come to find the hum of our neighbors' routines comforting.

Having the definitive purpose and structure of disciplined study before us has been elevating. There was no time wasted here. The hours we spent studying hard were rewarded with quiet evenings of reading books, coloring with our daughters, and taking walks. Days off school meant days and weekends of exploring the land as a family. Our time was so wonderfully defined with raising our kids, loving our neighbors, and studying hard. We must say good-bye even to the certitude of such purpose-driven structure, since we are days from being home and the Lord has not yet clarified our next steps.

While I can look back on our time here and see happy memories and a great deal of joy, I have not forgotten how painful the initial move was or the many challenges along the way. We lost two pregnancies this year, were stretched mentally and physically by our intensive studies, and missed out on key life moments with our families and friends back home that can never be relived. The cost of obedience has been high. But the Lord has been our shelter in every trial, and we have never more fully known how deep the Father's love for us.

As I slowly zip up another suitcase, I thank God for the hardships we can leave here like outgrown clothes, and I desperately cling to the intimacy that has resulted. It seems there is much to pray about, discern, and simply sort out.

But not tonight. It is *Shabbat*, the day we remember the Lord made the world and we did not. I will enjoy the quiet of the evening playing with the girls, take a walk, and have a long dinner with John. If there is one thing I would like to pack in my suitcase to ensure it comes home with us, it is the sacred sanctuary of *Shabbat*.

> Let us remember the way you led us in through the great and terrible wilderness, to test us, to know what was in our hearts, that you would do great and awesome things in our seeing. May we fear you, Lord, our God, may we serve you and cling to you.
>
> —from Deuteronomy 8–10

Lord, shelter us as we leave this desert we have loathed and loved. You alone know our path. We ask for the feet to walk it. Amen.

# Gratitude

I know I often skip the part of the book which lists an author's resources and sources of inspiration. Mostly they are no more than an unfamiliar roster of names and relationships. Yet I will unapologetically do something of the same. I must spend a moment giving thanks to my Lord as there are people in my life who have carried me through my time in the desert, and their love and encouragement have made our journey something worth sharing.

Lord, I bless You for John, my heart's partner in all things. His love and care for me truly reflect Your very best in this world. Can our Father's love for His children be more clearly portrayed than in his example?

I bless You for Brynn, Kate, and brand-new baby Meg. Their laughter inspires my days, and their wide-eyed, total dependence on me calls my attention to my own desperation for You. I am awe-struck that You would entrust them to me for a time. In Your sovereignty, You even orchestrated that the demands of our studies in Israel be perfectly met in the timing of their naps and their easy natures as babies and toddlers. They are true gifts and exceed every mother's hope. I pray they only ever know life swaddled in Your love.

I bless You for the little ones You put into my womb but I have yet to meet. I wouldn't have it any other way. You gave me the honor of carrying them for a time and the blessed assurance that they will only ever know the glory of Your presence. I am more eager than ever to join them someday, yet I pray You continually increase my anticipation of the best yet to come.

I bless You for our parents and grandparents, who never considered our surprising move to the Middle East to be anything but the right thing, and who never let us forget we were missed and loved. I praise You for our sisters and brothers, who sent stickers for the girls and prayed faithfully for our peace and safety.

I bless You for reaching into me through conversations with dear ones: Becky, Sue, Kris, and Cyndi. Thank You for speaking truth to my heart through Selena, Mindy, Cathy, and Dawn. Family time with the Burgesses and Kramers was a good and perfect gift.

I bless You for the encouraging words and prayers of our family at Richland Bible Church, and for leading us to the fellowship and friendships at Narkis Street Church. May we always and together seek first Your kingdom.

I bless You for the way You immediately granted us Mrs. Ruti's cozy apartment in Abu Tor, and for saying no when we wanted to move to Yemin Moshe. If we had gotten our way, we would never have known the love and hospitality of Ruth Joy and Frank.

I bless You for Jerusalem University College, namely the dedication of Paul and Diane Wright. Their sacrifices to stay have given us and countless others the amazing privilege of studying under such superb faculty. I am very grateful that Dr. Barkay honored my efforts with such kindness, never treating me like the novice student to the ancient Near East that

I am, and that Rabbi Moshe patiently endured my million questions.

I bless You for Your protective hand on our dear friend Jen, caretaker of our home and our Dugan. The friendships You provided in Lucas, Brent, Tom and Amy, Carrie, and Jen S. meant peace of mind in all matters while away from our home.

I bless You, Ancient of Days, for the appointed times You have purposed for us. I am especially grateful for Your drawing us into the sweetness of *Shabbat* every Friday evening and Saturday. I can now grasp the idea I have heard from many Jewish friends that we do not keep the *Shabbat* so much as it keeps us.

Lord, I ask that You continue to draw people into these sacred celebrations, and continue to provide ways our family can honor *Sukkot*. I believe You are delighted when we take time to be still, with friends, under the sky and under our tents, and together recall the ways You have sheltered us.

I bless You for our current season of waiting, for not allowing us to dive into some rigorous employment of our attention and affection. In Your perfect timing and grace, You have slowly introduced to us delightful projects from Your hand, good work You prepared ahead of time for us. Thank You for providing those who are committed to waiting, praying, and laboring alongside us.

Above all, I thank You for caring more about who we are than what we know, more about who we are becoming, than what we do.

Footnotes are a valuable tool to understand how an author's ideas came to be and I have frequently found remarkable insight at the very end of a book. While I cited sources appropriately, the uninterrupted and footnote-free narrative you just read was intended to allow ideas to develop according to the Lord's purposes, and to permit some queries to simply remain.

That said, I am deeply indebted to the work and skilled sharing of many, and sincerely grateful for the teachings and readings which inspired profoundly important questions in my life. Please take a moment to navigate

www.havingnothinglackingnothing.com

This website was developed to connect interested readers to resources the Lord has graciously put into place. I hope you find them instrumental in asking questions of our God who so lovingly and patiently pursues us. May He bless your every question with a more personal knowledge of His love and provision.

To order additional copies of this title call:
1-877-421-READ (7323)
or please visit our Web site at
www.winepressbooks.com

If you enjoyed this quality custom-published book,
drop by our Web site for more books and information.

www.winepressgroup.com
"Your partner in custom publishing."